I'M A WRITER!
(And I Didn't Even Know It)
Grade 1

By Teresa Domnauer

Frank Schaffer
An imprint of Carson-Dellosa Publishing LLC
PO Box 35665
Greensboro, NC 27425 USA

ISBN 978-0-7682-3961-4
196107784

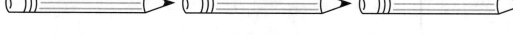

Table of Contents

Resources for Educators

Writing Activities

0-7682-3961-3 • I'm a Writer! Grade 1

Teacher Information

Dear Educator,

Congratulations on selecting the best in educational materials from Frank Schaffer Publications. The *I'm a Writer! (And I Didn't Even Know It)* series contains unique, fun, and creative writing activities designed to inspire young writers. Each activity is reproducible and self-contained, which makes them perfect for the classroom, home-schooling, or homework assignments. The activities are also divided into thematic sections so that you can easily correlate them with your current unit of study.

This book features activities for emerging writers. The activities are constructed of graphic organizers intended to guide students as they are just beginning to learn to write creatively. The activities are based on the print found in students' everyday worlds, such as food labels, posters, book covers, signs, and more. Students will have so much fun completing these activities that they won't even know they are writing!

On the following pages, you will find information especially for educators. Included are information about the writing process, creative writing ideas and prompts, a student writing checklist, and connections to national writing standards. You will also find a sample creative writing rubric, a blank rubric that can be customized for each writing assignment, and graphic organizers, which are blank and can be used over and over again for various lessons.

The activities in this book are designed to be fun, to help nurture students' creativity, and to meet important education standards for language arts. Incorporate the *I'm a Writer! (And I Didn't Even Know It)* series into your classroom and watch your students flourish as writers!

Sincerely,
Frank Schaffer Publications

© Carson-Dellosa

0-7682-3961-3 • I'm a Writer! Grade 1

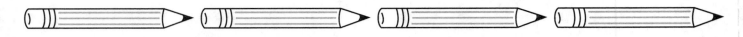

The Writing Process

Many first-grade students are developing writers. They are learning to convey ideas by writing words, phrases, sentences, and short paragraphs. They are drawing, dictating, and describing orally. They are beginning to recognize, read, and write high-frequency words, and they are learning to build words and word families. The activities in this book focus on getting developing writers to generate ideas related to a topic, which is the foundation for prewriting. The activities also allow students to begin to elaborate on the topic.

During the school year, your students will grow and develop as writers. You can encourage this by helping them learn how to plan their writing with prewriting and drafting, revise and edit their writing by making corrections and changes, and publish their writing in a polished format. This is all part of the writing process. It also might be helpful to explain the five steps of the writing process to your students.

Prewriting
Prewriting is what you do before you write. It is a way of collecting your thoughts and ideas on what you want to write about. Sometimes, it is called *brainstorming*. You can prewrite by drawing pictures, making lists, or writing sentences or sentence parts.

Drafting
Your first try at writing about a topic is called a *rough draft*. When you write a rough draft, don't worry about spelling and punctuation—just get your writing started.

Revising
Revising means making corrections. When you revise your writing, you want to be sure it makes sense. You want to make sure that nothing is missing. This is also a good time to check that you have used interesting words.

Proofreading
When you proofread your writing, you look for mistakes. Now, it is time to check your spelling and punctuation and to make sure you capitalized words correctly.

Publishing
When you publish your writing, you are ready for people to read it! You should use your best handwriting and a clean sheet of paper. You also can type what you have written on a computer and print it out.

Name _____   Date _____

Story Web: Beginning, Middle, and End

Beginning	Middle	End

0-7682-3961-3 • I'm a Writer! Grade 1

Name _____   Date _____

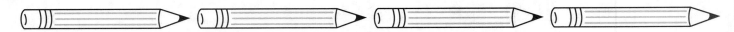

Story Web: Character, Setting, Problem, Solution

Characters	Setting
Problem	**Solution**

0-7682-3961-3 • I'm a Writer! Grade 1

Writing Web

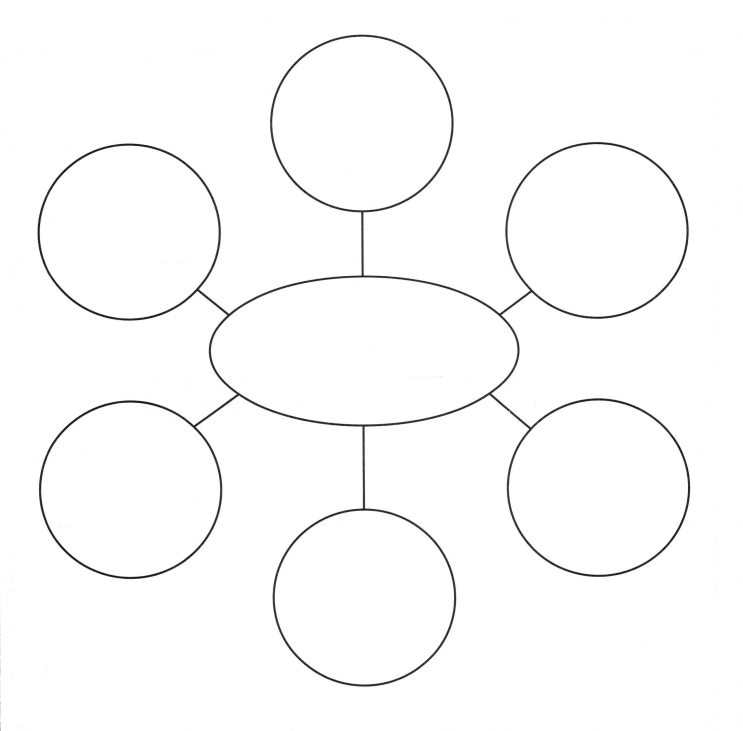

0-7682-3961-3 • I'm a Writer! Grade 1

Creative Writing Practice Page

Use this page for extra writing and drawing practice.

0-7682-3961-3 • I'm a Writer! Grade 1

Writing Checklist for Students

☐ Did I write my name at the top of the paper?

☐ Did I begin all of my sentences with a capital letter?

☐ Did I end all of my sentences with punctuation?

☐ Did I use capital letters at the beginning of names and other proper nouns?

☐ Do all of my sentences state a complete thought?

☐ Did I double-check the words that I wasn't sure how to spell?

☐ Are all of my words and letters sitting on the writing line?

☐ Are all of my words clear and easy to read?

0-7682-3961-3 • I'm a Writer! Grade 1

Connections to National Writing Standards

The activities in *I'm a Writer! (And I Didn't Even Know It)* are specifically designed to meet national standards for writing:

- Students will use skills and strategies related to the writing process.
- Students will use drawings to express their thoughts, feelings, and ideas.
- Students will use descriptive words to share their ideas.
- Students will evaluate their own writing and that of their peers, including offering constructive criticism and helping with grammar and spelling.
- Students will use a variety of writing forms, including letters, stories, lists, webs, and invitations.
- Students will engage in prewriting to plan their writing. This includes discussing ideas with their peers.
- Students will organize their writing, including sequencing events.
- Students will write for different purposes, such as to entertain, to inform, to learn, and to communicate.
- Students will draw, write, and dictate to describe familiar persons, places, objects, and experiences.
- Students will use a variety of sentence types, including statements, questions, and exclamations.
- Students will orient their writing from left to right and from top to bottom. They will use uppercase and lowercase letters and space words and sentences.
- Students will write complete sentences that include nouns, verbs, adjectives, and adverbs.
- Students will use appropriate capitalization and punctuation.
- Students will use a variety of strategies to spell words.

Additional Suggestions

- Take the opportunity to tie in a piece of literature related to each writing activity.
- Discuss that writing is found all around students—in books, on signs, on grocery packages, on television, in the newspaper, and more.
- Encourage developing writers to sound out words and to use a dictionary to help them with spelling. Students can also work with partners or in small groups to evaluate each other's writing and to assist each other with grammar and spelling.
- Incorporate an art project with a writing activity, such as decorating empty cardboard boxes to look like food products or toys.
- Use the Story Web on page 6 to introduce literary elements, including characters, setting, problem, and solution. Students can use this web to plan their own stories or to dissect stories that they have read in class.

Creative Writing Suggestions

- Set up a writing center in your classroom. Supply the area with pencils, crayons, markers, erasers, a variety of papers, blank postcards, blank greeting cards, envelopes, a cookie sheet with magnetic letters, age-appropriate scissors, and non-toxic glue sticks. Post student writing on the walls for classmates to enjoy.
- Before beginning a writing activity, brainstorm with students as a whole group. Write their ideas on chart paper and model the writing activity for them. You may also wish to bring in items related to the activity, such as an invitation, a postcard, an envelope, a soup can, or a candy wrapper. Students can bring in related items, such as a picture of a favorite sports hero.
- The day before a writing activity, encourage students to go home and think over the topic about which they will be writing. This will allow time for the ideas to churn around in students' minds. It's like subconscious prewriting!
- For developing writers, you might want to write a sentence starter for students to copy onto the activity page.
- Support struggling writers by acting as a scribe as they dictate their ideas to you.
- When students complete their writing assignments, allow time for oral presentations.
- Compile a writing portfolio for each student that contains examples of his or her best pieces. Involve the students in choosing the writing for their portfolios.
- Give students opportunities to publish finished pieces of writing on the computer.
- Compile a classroom book with a piece of writing from each student. Place the book in your writing center so that students may read it.
- To introduce and model webbing, copy the writing web on page 7 onto chart paper. Have students generate a list of items as you complete the web. Have students complete a similar web on their own using copies of the writing web.
- Provide journals and offer journal activities for students each day. Make sure students write the date on each page. At the end of the school year, students can see how their writing has improved. The journal is also an excellent place for students to brainstorm topics they would like to write about in the future.

Creative Writing Prompts

- Read a fairy tale to the class. Have students write and draw about what happens next or how they could change the ending.
- Have students write about a dream, a memory, or a time when they were sad, happy, or angry.
- Have students write about something they are afraid of.
- Have students write about a grandparent, a vacation, or a time when they made someone happy.

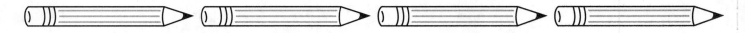

Creative Writing Scoring Rubric

This rubric gives some ideas on how to evaluate a child's early writing work. Rubrics can be created in the same manner for any assignment. Rubrics make the objectives clear, and scoring illustrates a child's level of achievement relative to the objectives.

Objectives	Points Awarded		
	1 point	**3 points**	**5 points**
Number of sentences written	1 or 2	3 or 4	5 or more
Writing adheres to instructions given regarding content	Does not	Somewhat	Does
Writing includes punctuation at the end of each sentence	1 or 2 sentences have punctuation	2 or 3 sentences have punctuation	4 or more sentences have punctuation
Sentences begin with capital letters	1 or 2 sentences do	2 or 3 sentences do	4 or more sentences do

Total Score: _____ out of 20 possible points.

Here are some additional objectives you may wish to include on rubrics:
- Student listened while instructions were being given.
- Student followed directions.
- Student worked independently.
- Student took his or her time and did not rush through the activity.
- Student indicated understanding of objective of activity.
- Student stayed on task.
- Student used invented spelling.
- Student attempted to write words.
- Student attempted to write a sentence (or sentences).
- Student wrote complete sentences.
- Student wrote name on paper.
- Student filled the page.
- Student used punctuation.
- Student used capital letters when appropriate.
- Student completed entire assignment.

0-7682-3961-3 • I'm a Writer! Grade 1

Rubric

Rubric For: _____

Objectives	Points Awarded		
	_____point(s)	_____point(s)	_____point(s)

Total Score: _____ out of _____ possible points.

0-7682-3961-3 • I'm a Writer! Grade 1

Family Photo Album

Directions: Draw your family members in the photo album. Write each person's name below the photo.

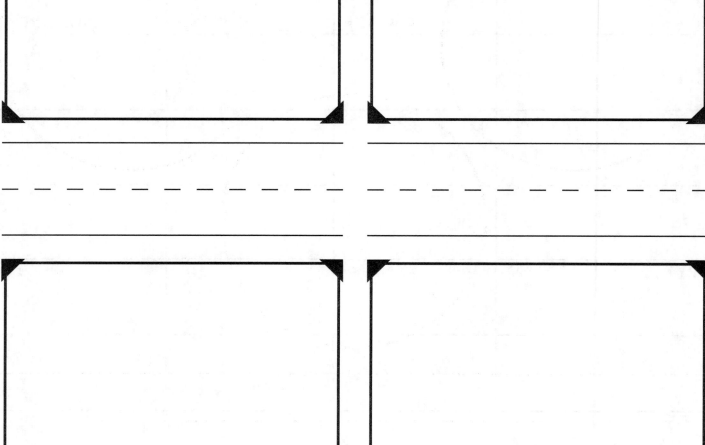

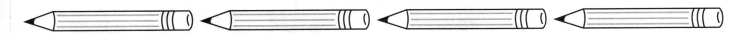

My Kind of Fun

Directions: In each circle, draw one of your favorite things to do. Write a sentence about one of your favorite activities on the lines.

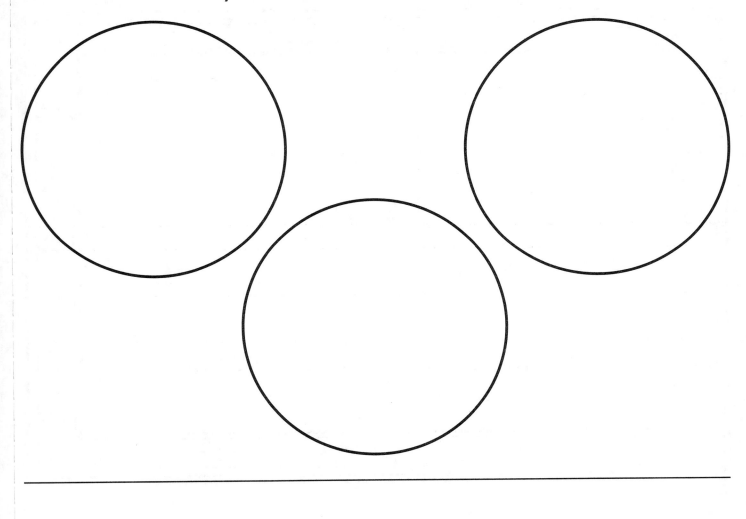

0-7682-3961-3 • I'm a Writer! Grade 1

Proud of Myself

Directions: Draw a picture of a time when you were proud of yourself. Write a sentence about your picture on the lines.

_ _

_____

_ _

_____

0-7682-3961-3 • I'm a Writer! Grade 1

My Wish

Directions: Draw a picture of a wish that you have. Write a sentence about your wish on the lines.

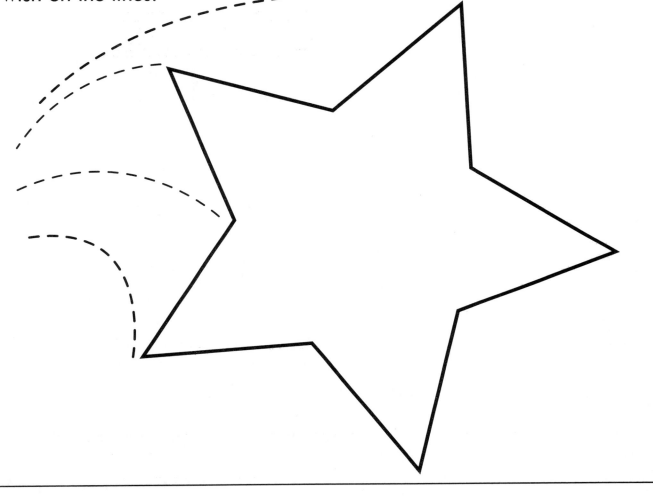

0-7682-3961-3 • I'm a Writer! Grade 1

When I Grow Up

Directions: Draw a picture of yourself as a grown-up. Show what you would like to be or to do. Write a sentence about your picture on the lines.

0-7682-3961-3 • I'm a Writer! Grade 1

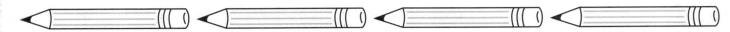

My Neighborhood

Directions: Do you live in a city, on a farm, or in a small town? Draw a picture of your neighborhood. Then, write a sentence about your picture on the lines.

Home Sweet Home

_____

_____

_____

_____

0-7682-3961-3 • I'm a Writer! Grade 1

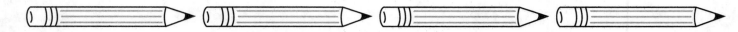

Grocery List

Directions: It is time to go shopping! What would you like to buy at the grocery store? Write a list of the foods you would choose.

0-7682-3961-3 • I'm a Writer! Grade 1

Soup Can

Directions: Draw a label for this can of soup. Write the name of the soup on the can. Then, write some of the ingredients in the soup on the lines.

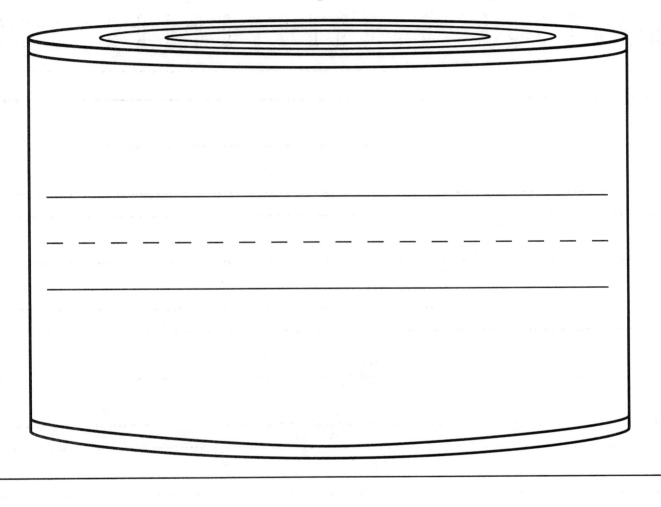

0-7682-3961-3 • I'm a Writer! Grade 1

Cereal Box

Directions: This is your chance to invent your own breakfast cereal! Design a box for your cereal. Write the name of the cereal on the box. Then, write a sentence about your cereal on the lines.

0-7682-3961-3 • I'm a Writer! Grade 1

Candy Wrapper

Directions: Dream up your own candy bar! Decorate the wrapper below. Don't forget to write the name of the candy bar on the wrapper. Then, write a sentence about your candy on the lines.

    0-7682-3961-3 • I'm a Writer! Grade 1

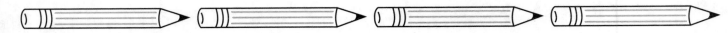

Feast for a Pet

Directions: Draw a special meal for your pet. If you don't have a pet, draw a meal for an imaginary pet. Then, write a sentence about your pet's feast on the lines.

0-7682-3961-3 • I'm a Writer! Grade 1

One Delicious Recipe

Directions: What is your favorite kind of cookie? How do you think this cookie is made? Write the recipe for your favorite cookie. Don't forget to write the baking instructions.

Recipe for:

0-7682-3961-3 • I'm a Writer! Grade 1

Restaurant Menu

Directions: Design your own restaurant menu. Draw the foods you would like to have on the menu for breakfast, lunch, and dinner. Write the name of a food for each meal.

Menu

Breakfast

_____

- -

_____

0-7682-3961-3 • I'm a Writer! Grade 1

Lunch

Dinner

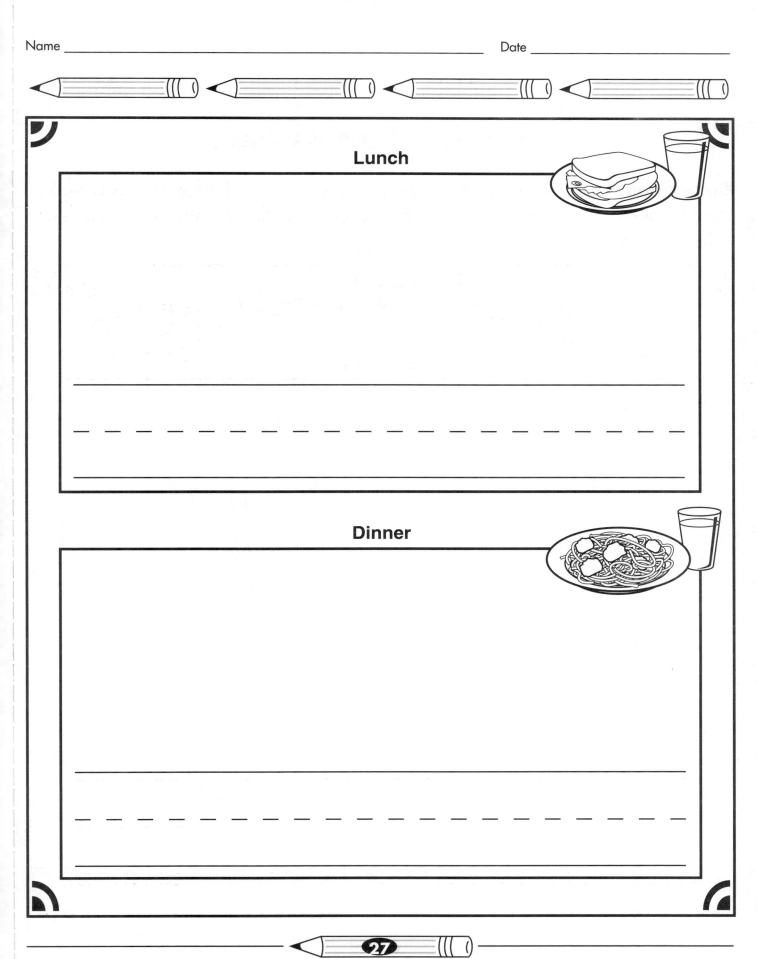

0-7682-3961-3 • I'm a Writer! Grade 1

Me as a Sports Star

Directions: Imagine yourself as a sports star. Draw a picture of yourself on the trading card. Write a sentence about yourself on the lines.

Sports Star

_____

- -

_____

- -

_____

0-7682-3961-3 • I'm a Writer! Grade 1

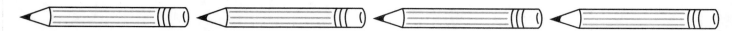

My Hero

Directions: Draw a picture of a person who you think is a hero. Write a sentence about your hero on the lines.

- -

- -

- -

0-7682-3961-3 • I'm a Writer! Grade 1

Letter to My Hero

Directions: Now, write a letter to your hero. Tell the person why you think he or she is a hero. Be sure to include the date, a greeting, a message, and a closing and signature.

(Date)

(Greeting)

(Body)

(Closing)

(Signature—your name)

0-7682-3961-3 • I'm a Writer! Grade 1

Name _____   Date _____

My Favorite Superhero

Directions: Who is your favorite superhero? Draw a picture of him or her. Write a sentence about the superhero on the lines.

_____

- -

_____

- -

_____

0-7682-3961-3 • I'm a Writer! Grade 1

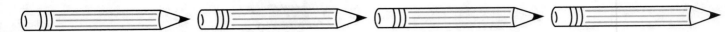

I'm a Superhero!

Directions: Now, imagine yourself as a superhero. What superpowers do you have? Draw yourself as a superhero. Write a sentence about your superpowers on the lines.

_____

- -

_____

_____

- -

_____

Make a Monster

Directions: Monsters can come in all shapes, sizes, and colors! Draw a monster that you imagine. Write a sentence about the monster on the lines.

_____

- -

_____

- -

_____

0-7682-3961-3 • I'm a Writer! Grade 1

My Favorite Cartoon Character

Directions: Draw your favorite cartoon character inside the television. Write a sentence about the character on the lines.

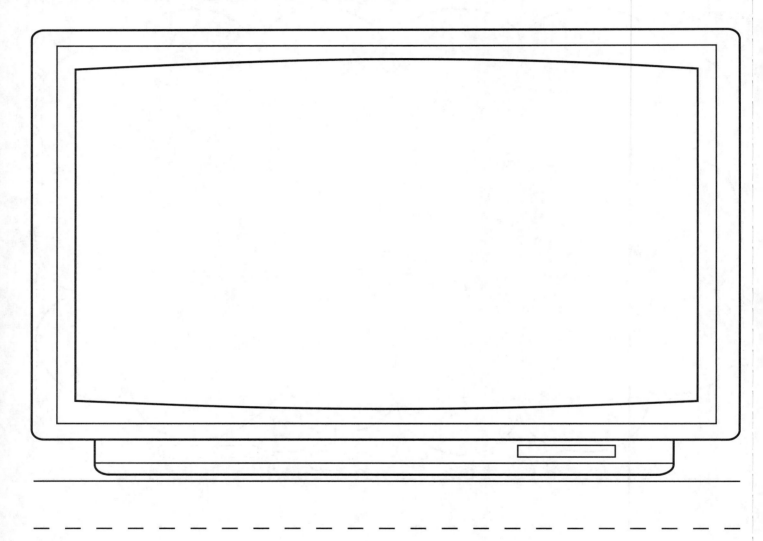

- -

_____

- -

_____

34

Cartoon Show

Directions: What is your favorite cartoon show? Draw an event that happened on your favorite cartoon show. Write a sentence about the show on the lines.

35

Invent a Pen Pal

Directions: Imagine that you could write to a friend your age in another part of the world. Draw a picture of your imaginary pen pal. Then, write a sentence about him or her on the lines.

_____

- -

_____

- -

_____

0-7682-3961-3 • I'm a Writer! Grade 1

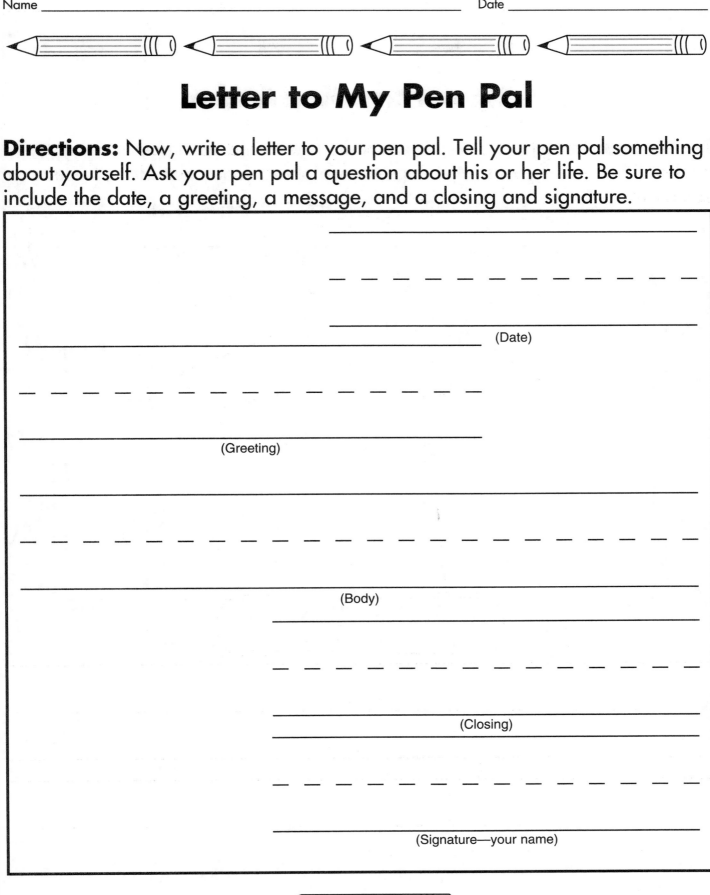

Letter to My Pen Pal

Directions: Now, write a letter to your pen pal. Tell your pen pal something about yourself. Ask your pen pal a question about his or her life. Be sure to include the date, a greeting, a message, and a closing and signature.

(Date)

(Greeting)

(Body)

(Closing)

(Signature—your name)

0-7682-3961-3 • I'm a Writer! Grade 1

Name _____   Date _____

I'm a Famous Artist

Directions: Imagine that you are a famous artist. Draw a painting that you think will become famous. Write a sentence about your painting on the lines

     0-7682-3961-3 • I'm a Writer! Grade 1

The Music in Me

Directions: Is there a musical instrument that you wish you could play? Draw a picture of it. Then, write a sentence about why you'd like to play this instrument on the lines.

The Dancer in Me

Directions: Imagine yourself as a dancer on stage. Draw a picture of your performance. Then, write a sentence about the show on the lines.

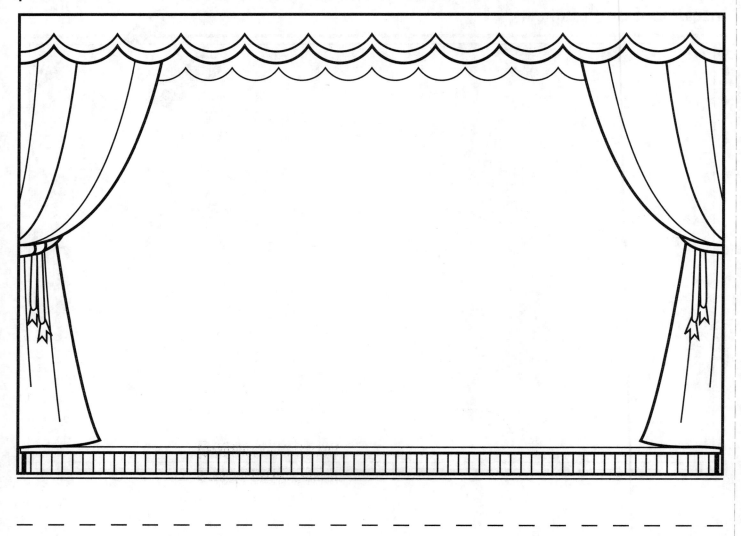

_____

_____

_____

_____

0-7682-3961-3 • I'm a Writer! Grade 1

Cinderella on Stage

Directions: Think of the characters in the story *Cinderella*. Draw a costume for one of the characters. Then, write a sentence about the character on the lines.

_____

- -

_____

- -

_____

0-7682-3961-3 • I'm a Writer! Grade 1

CD Cover

Directions: What is your favorite musical group? Design a CD cover for your group's next CD. Be sure to include the name of the group. Then, write a sentence about the music on the lines.

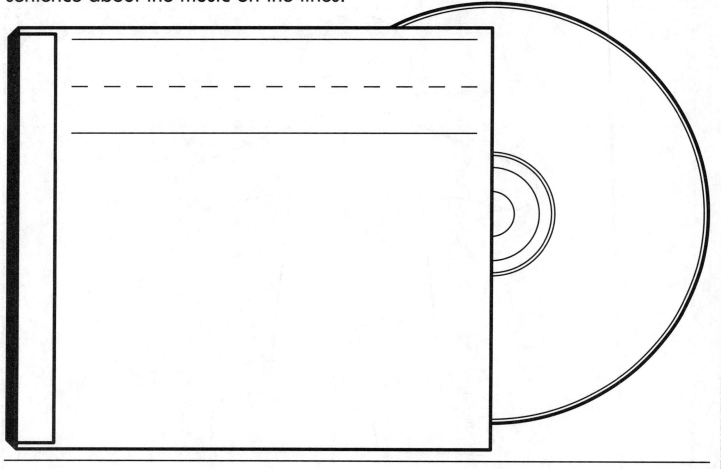

_____

_ _

_____

_____

0-7682-3961-3 • I'm a Writer! Grade 1

Circus Poster

Directions: Imagine that the circus is coming to your town! Create a poster that tells about the circus. Be sure to include the name of the circus and the date, time, and place.

Time

Place   **Date**

    0-7682-3961-3 • I'm a Writer! Grade 1

Silly Book Cover

Directions: Design a cover for a book with a very silly story. Be sure to include the title of the book and the author and illustrator.

Author _____

Illustrator _____

0-7682-3961-3 • I'm a Writer! Grade 1

Healthy Me

Directions: What are some things that you do to stay healthy? Draw four ways that you stay healthy. Then, write a sentence about one of your pictures on the lines.

0-7682-3961-3 • I'm a Writer! Grade 1

Healthy Snacks

Directions: Draw some healthy snacks on the plate. Then, write a sentence about the snacks on the lines.

0-7682-3961-3 • I'm a Writer! Grade 1

When I'm Sick

Directions: When you are sick, what makes you feel better? Draw a picture of something that helps you feel better. Then, write a sentence about your picture on the lines.

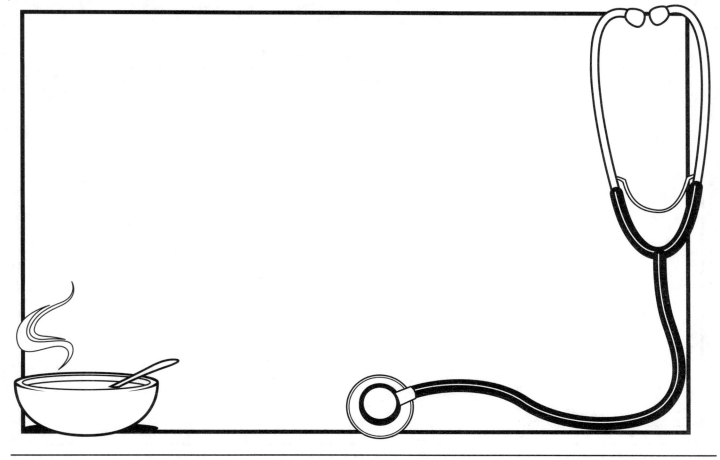

0-7682-3961-3 • I'm a Writer! Grade 1

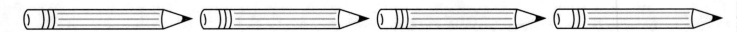

A Doctor's Kit

Directions: What tools does a doctor use? Draw the tools in the doctor's bag. Then, write a sentence about a doctor on the lines.

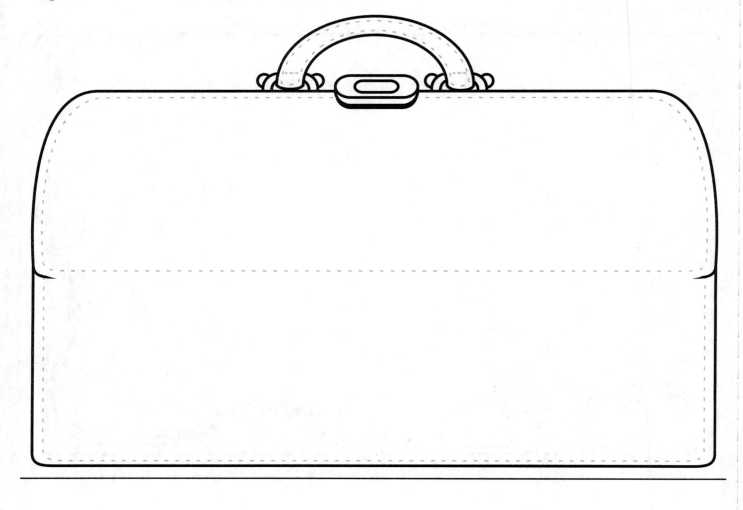

0-7682-3961-3 • I'm a Writer! Grade 1

Exercise

Directions: Getting exercise is fun and healthy. Draw a picture that shows your favorite exercise. Then, write a sentence about your picture on the lines.

_____

_____

_____

_____

0-7682-3961-3 • I'm a Writer! Grade 1

Terrific Tennis Shoes

Directions: Tennis shoes are great to wear when you exercise. Design your own pair of tennis shoes. Write a sentence about your shoes on the lines.

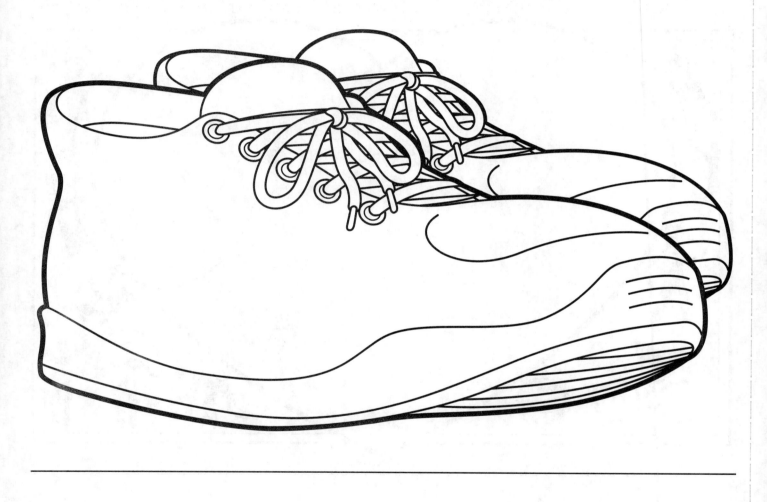

0-7682-3961-3 • I'm a Writer! Grade 1

Emotions

Directions: Emotions are the different ways that we feel. How many emotions can you think of? Draw a different one on each face. Circle the face that shows how you feel today. Then, write a sentence about how you feel on the lines.

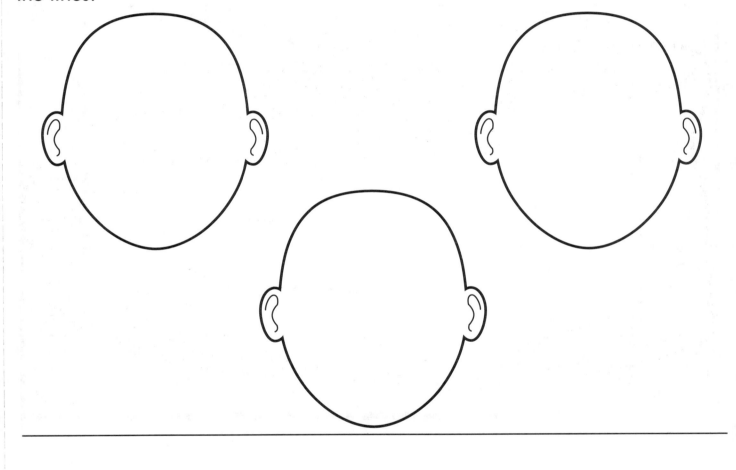

0-7682-3961-3 • I'm a Writer! Grade 1

Emotions

Directions: Choose an emotion from the previous page. Draw a picture of a time when you felt this emotion. Then, write a sentence about your picture on the lines.

- -

_____

_____

- -

_____

0-7682-3961-3 • I'm a Writer! Grade 1

Being Safe

Directions: There are many things you can do to stay safe. Draw a picture of one thing you do to stay safe. Then, write a sentence about your picture on the lines.

_____

- -

_____

_____

- -

_____

0-7682-3961-3 • I'm a Writer! Grade 1

Danger Ahead!

Directions: Signs help warn people about danger. Make your own sign that will tell people about something dangerous. Write a sentence about the danger on the lines.

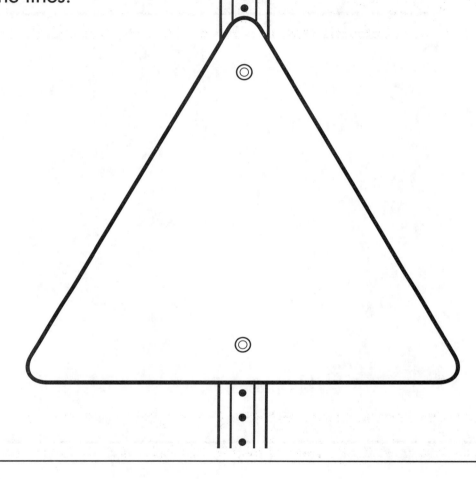

© Carson-Dellosa   0-7682-3961-3 • I'm a Writer! Grade 1

Celebrations

Directions: Think of a celebration that is special to your family. Draw a picture of the celebration. Then, write a sentence about it on the lines.

_ _

_____

_____

_ _

_____

0-7682-3961-3 • I'm a Writer! Grade 1

Invitation to a Costume Party

Directions: Imagine that you are having a costume party. Decorate the invitation. Write your address on it. Then, write the date and time of your party. Read the invitation out loud to a friend.

Please come to my costume party!

Address

_____

- - - - - - - - - - - - - - - - - - -

Date

_____

- - - - - - - - - - - - - - - - - - -

Time

_____

- - - - - - - - - - - - - - - - - - -

_____

0-7682-3961-3 • I'm a Writer! Grade 1

Design a Costume

Directions: Now, design a costume to wear to your party. Write a sentence about your costume on the lines.

0-7682-3961-3 • I'm a Writer! Grade 1

Movie Poster

Directions: Think about your favorite movie. Draw a poster for the movie. Write the name of the movie on the poster. Then, write a sentence about the movie on the lines.

0-7682-3961-3 • I'm a Writer! Grade 1

Popcorn

Directions: Popcorn is a favorite movie treat. Write the word *popcorn* on the container. Then, decorate the container. Be sure to add the popcorn! Write a sentence about the popcorn on the lines.

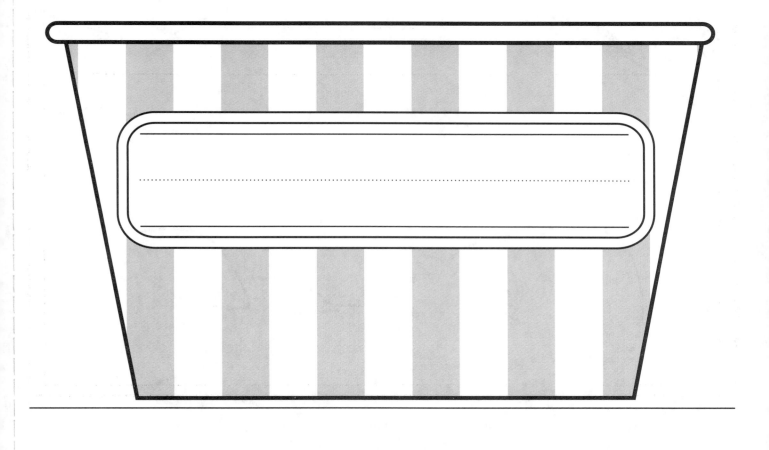

0-7682-3961-3 • I'm a Writer! Grade 1

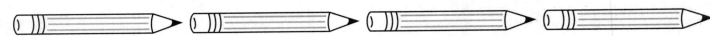

Amusement Park Map

Directions: Have you ever been to an amusement park? Now, you can design your own. Draw the rides and games that you would like to have at your very own amusement park. Write a sentence about your park on the lines.

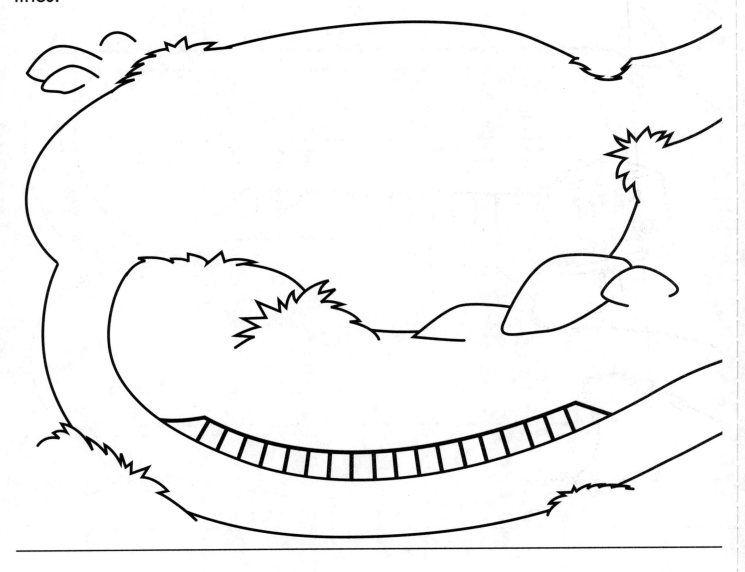

0-7682-3961-3 • I'm a Writer! Grade 1

FUN
PARK

Video Game

Directions: What is your favorite video or computer game? Draw a picture of the game on the screen below. Then, write a sentence about the game on the lines.

My Own Video Game

Directions: Now, make up your own video or computer game. Draw a picture of the game on the screen below. Then, write a sentence about the game on the lines.

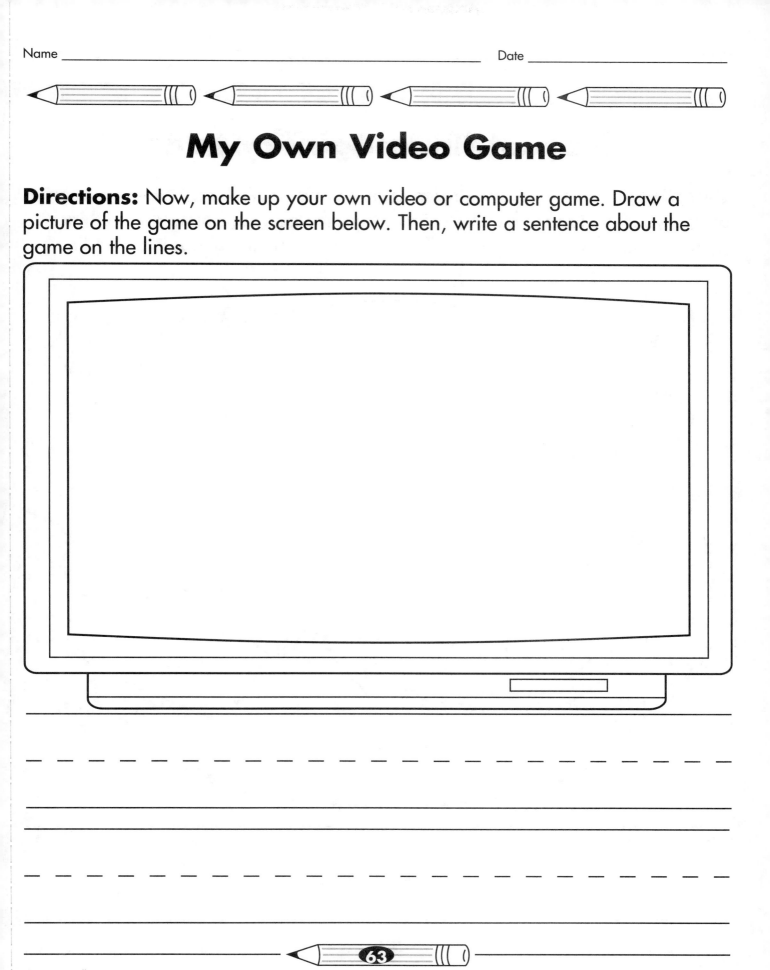

0-7682-3961-3 • I'm a Writer! Grade 1

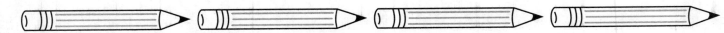

Map of an Imaginary Land

Directions: Have you ever dreamed of an imaginary land? Now, you can design your own make-believe place. Draw the people, animals, and things that you would see in this place. Then, write a sentence about it on the lines.

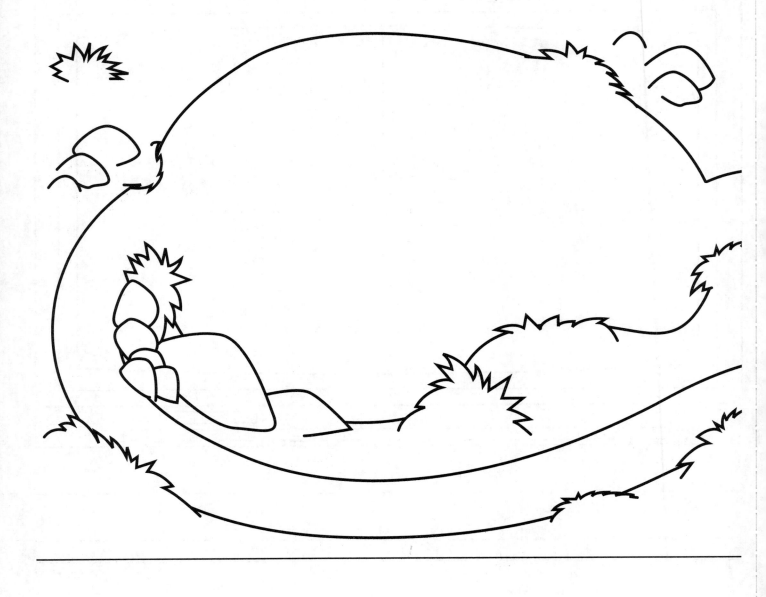

_____

– –

_____

0-7682-3961-3 • I'm a Writer! Grade 1

0-7682-3961-3 • I'm a Writer! Grade 1

Name _____   Date _____

Puppet Show

Directions: Draw a puppet show on the stage. Write a sentence about the puppet show on the lines.

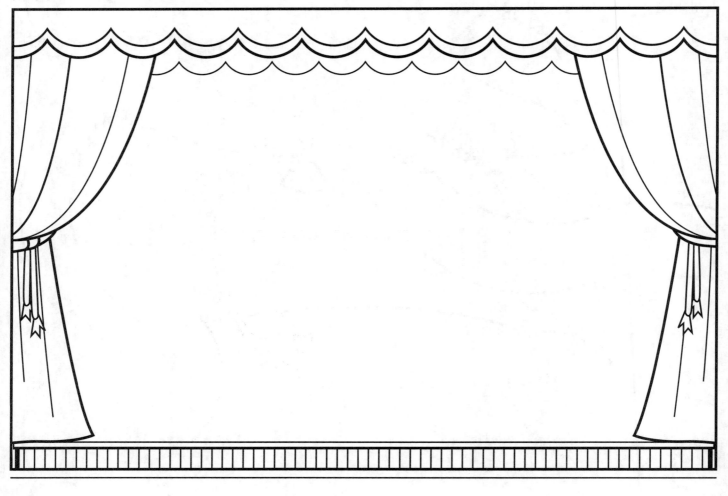

- -

_____

- -

_____

0-7682-3961-3 • I'm a Writer! Grade 1

Australian Animals

Directions: Australia is filled with unique and amazing animals. Draw four Australian animals in the web below. Then, write a sentence about them on the lines.

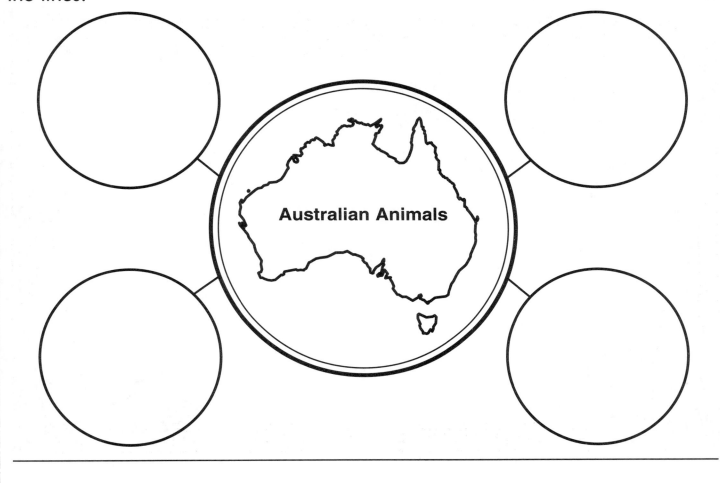

Australian Animals

_____

_ _

_____

_ _

_____

0-7682-3961-3 • I'm a Writer! Grade 1

The Rain Forest

Directions: Many unusual plants and animals live in the rain forest. Draw your favorite rain forest animals in the scene below. Then, write a sentence about them on the lines.

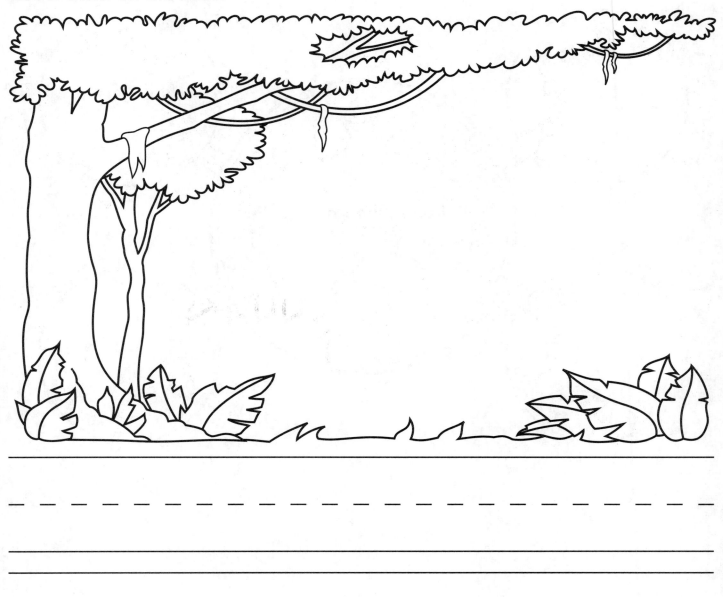

_____

_ _

_____

_ _

_____

0-7682-3961-3 • I'm a Writer! Grade 1

Arctic Animals

Directions: Arctic animals live in a harsh and cold climate. Draw four Arctic animals in the web below. Then, write a sentence about them on the lines.

**Arctic
Animals**

_____

_ _

_____

_____

_ _

_____

0-7682-3961-3 • I'm a Writer! Grade 1

Reptiles

Directions: What makes reptiles different from other animals? Write a list of things that make reptiles unique. Then, draw your favorite reptile.

Amphibians

Directions: What makes amphibians different from other animals? Write a list of things that make amphibians unique. Then, draw your favorite amphibian.

Mammals

Directions: What makes mammals different from other animals? Write a list of things that make mammals unique. Then, draw your favorite mammal.

0-7682-3961-3 • I'm a Writer! Grade 1

Insects

Directions: What makes insects different from other animals? Write a list of things that make insects unique. Then, draw your favorite insect.

_____

- -

_____

_____

- -

_____

_____

- -

_____

_____

- -

_____

0-7682-3961-3 • I'm a Writer! Grade 1

Zoo Map

Directions: Use this page to design your own zoo. Draw the animals that you would like to have at the zoo. Write a sentence about your zoo on the lines.

_____

- -

_____

0-7682-3961-3 • I'm a Writer! Grade 1

0-7682-3961-3 • I'm a Writer! Grade 1

Shark Tank!

Directions: Imagine that you work at an aquarium. Draw a sign for the shark tank. Add words to the sign that will tell visitors about sharks.

0-7682-3961-3 • I'm a Writer! Grade 1

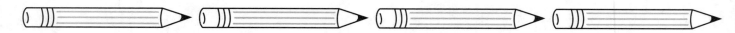

My Robot

Directions: Use this page to design your own robot. Draw a picture of your robot and label its parts. Write the name of your robot at the bottom of the page.

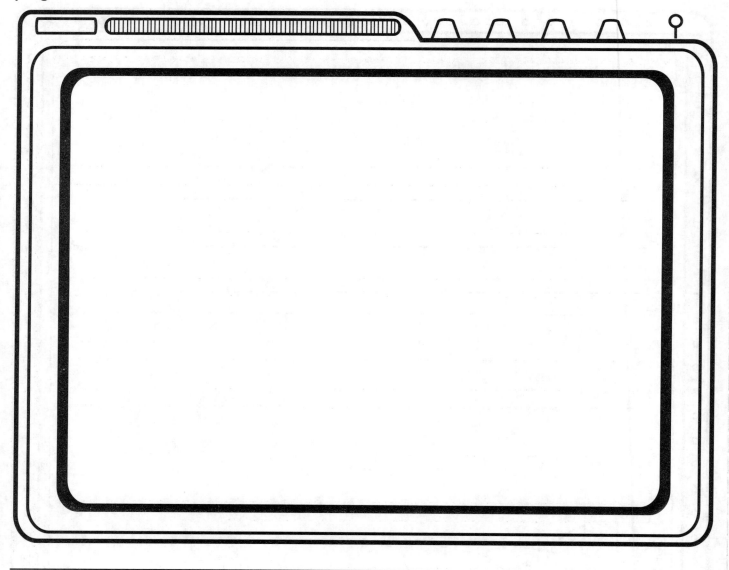

0-7682-3961-3 • I'm a Writer! Grade 1

Look What My Robot Can Do!

Directions: Now, write a list of all the amazing things your robot can do. Imagine that you are going to make hundreds of these robots to sell. Make sure your list includes things that will make people want to buy it.

0-7682-3961-3 • I'm a Writer! Grade 1

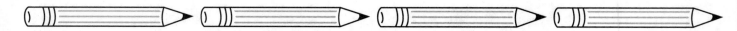

Envelope

Directions: Write your name and address on the envelope.

Name:

Address:

BOSTON
OCT 7
6-PM
18 98
MASS.

0-7682-3961-3 • I'm a Writer! Grade 1

Postcard

Directions: Have you ever sent a postcard? Have you ever gotten one in the mail? People often send postcards when they are on vacation. Draw a picture on the postcard. Show a place you would like to visit. Write a sentence about the place on the lines.

Postage Stamp

Directions: Postage stamps come in many different designs. They have animals, people, and even cartoon characters on them! Design your own postage stamp. Write the amount of money that the stamp will cost. Then, write a sentence about your stamp on the lines.

¢

_____

_____

_____

_____

0-7682-3961-3 • I'm a Writer! Grade 1

Cool Computers

Directions: Computers help people in many ways. Draw one way that a computer can help you. Write a sentence about your picture on the lines.

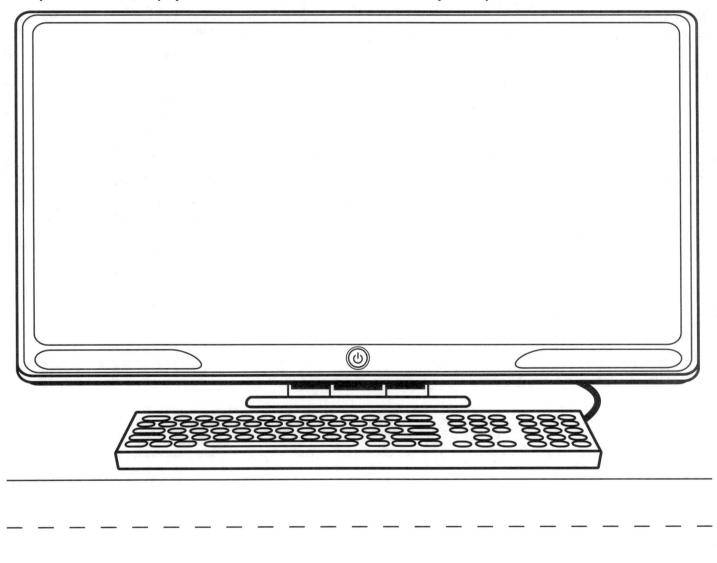

- -

_____

- -

_____

    0-7682-3961-3 • I'm a Writer! Grade 1

Name _____ Date _____

Zoo Sign

Directions: Signs are everywhere, and they often give important information. Draw a sign that you might see at a zoo. Add words to the sign to help people understand what the sign is about.

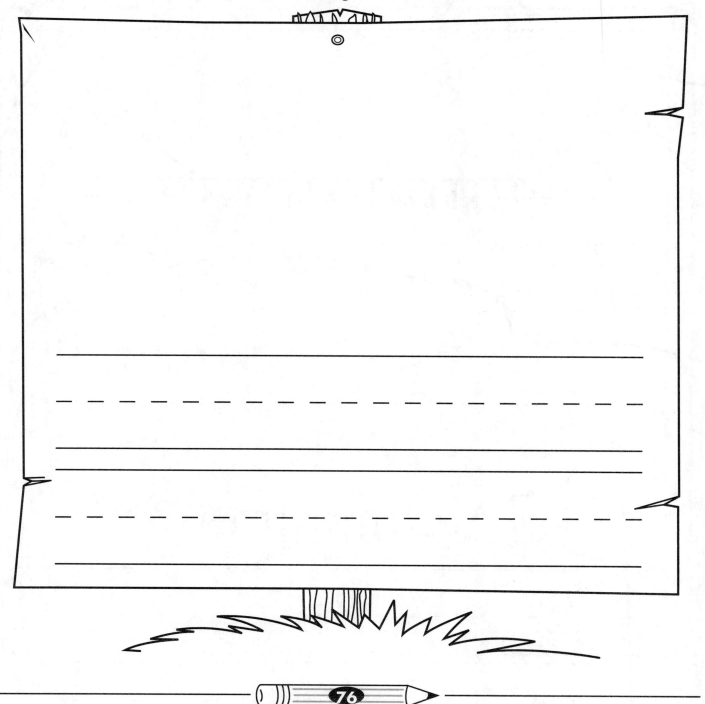

                    0-7682-3961-3 • I'm a Writer! Grade 1

Booting Up

Directions: Imagine that you have a friend who has never used a computer. Write the steps to tell your friend how to turn on the computer and get started.

0-7682-3961-3 • I'm a Writer! Grade 1

Name _____   Date _____

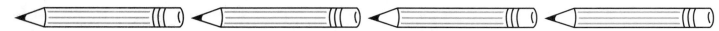

Calendar

Directions: Fill in the calendar for this month. Write the name of the month at the top. Write the number of days. Decorate the boxes of any holidays or special days!

					SUNDAY
					MONDAY
					TUESDAY
					WEDNESDAY
					THURSDAY
					FRIDAY
					SATURDAY

0-7682-3961-3 • I'm a Writer! Grade 1

Cool Coins

Directions: Here is your chance to design your own money! Decorate the nickel, dime, and quarter. Write a sentence about your coins on the lines.

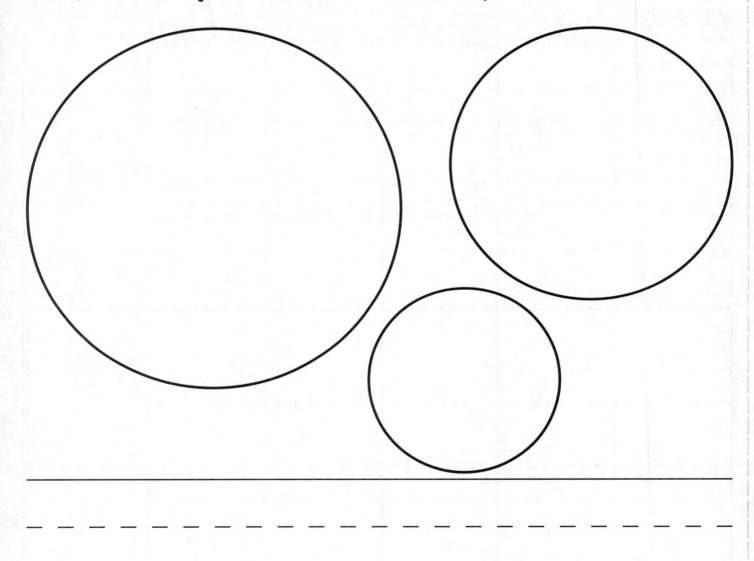

_____

- -

_____

- -

_____

0-7682-3961-3 • I'm a Writer! Grade 1

Write Your Own Addition Problem

Directions: People use math everyday. They use it at the grocery store, while cooking, and even while playing cards or video games! Write your own story problem that uses addition. Then, write the answer to the problem in the box. Write a sentence that tells how to solve the problem. Draw pictures if it helps you.

0-7682-3961-3 • I'm a Writer! Grade 1

Write Your Own Subtraction Problem

Directions: People use math everyday. They use it at the grocery store, while cooking, and even while playing cards or video games! Write your own story problem that uses subtraction. Then, write the answer to the problem in the box. Write a sentence that tells how to solve the problem. Draw pictures if it helps you.

0-7682-3961-3 • I'm a Writer! Grade 1

Shape Up

Directions: Draw a picture using only shapes. Then, write the names of some of the shapes that you used.

_____

_ _

_____

_____

_ _

_____

0-7682-3961-3 • I'm a Writer! Grade 1

Smallest to Largest

Directions: Draw four animals, ranging in size from smallest to largest. Write a sentence about one of the animals on the lines.

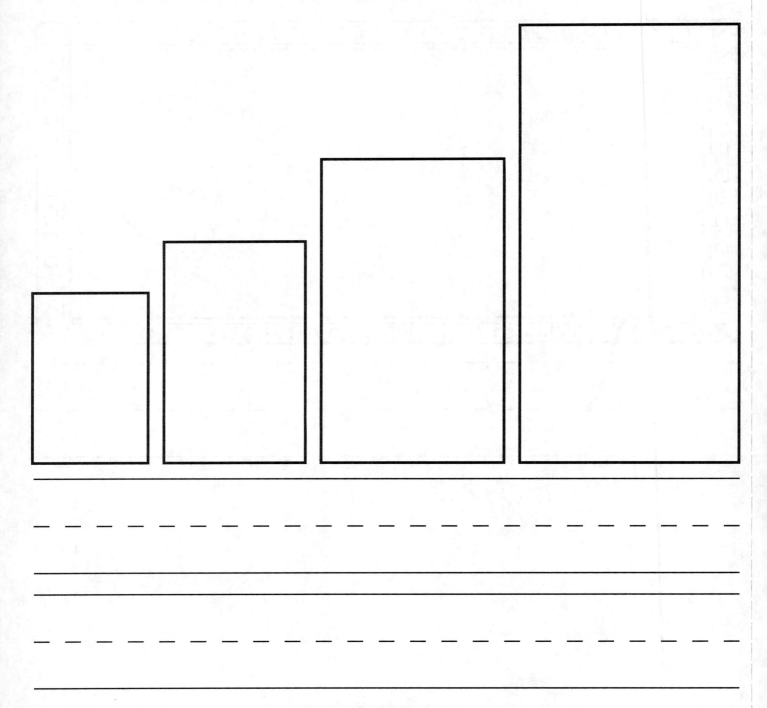

Helping Hand

Directions: How do you help other people? Draw one way that you can help others. Then, write a sentence about helping others on the lines.

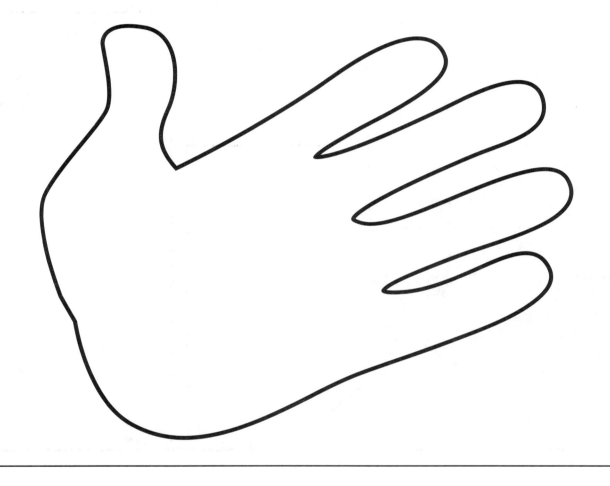

0-7682-3961-3 • I'm a Writer! Grade 1

Helping the Planet

Directions: How can you take care of the Earth? Draw one way that you help the planet. Write a sentence about your picture on the lines.

0-7682-3961-3 • I'm a Writer! Grade 1

Recipe for a Peaceful Planet

Directions: What do you think it would take to make a peaceful planet? Write a "recipe" of your ideas. For example, you might write "a cup of friendship."

Recipe for a Peaceful Planet

0-7682-3961-3 • I'm a Writer! Grade 1

Recipe for a Peaceful Classroom

Directions: What do you think it would take to make a peaceful classroom? Write a "recipe" of your ideas. For example, you might write "a spoonful of kindness."

Recipe for a Peaceful Classroom

0-7682-3961-3 • I'm a Writer! Grade 1

Saving Endangered Animals

Directions: How can people help endangered animals? Draw a poster that shows one way you think people could help. Write a sentence about your idea on the lines.

0-7682-3961-3 • I'm a Writer! Grade 1

Stopping Pollution

Directions: How can people stop pollution? Draw a poster that shows one way you think people could help keep the planet clean. Write a sentence about your idea on the lines.

0-7682-3961-3 • I'm a Writer! Grade 1